Flora Flamingo Learns to Fly

by Maria Fleming
illustrated by Kellie Lewis

SCHOLASTIC INC.

New York • Toronto • London • Auckland • Sydney
Mexico City • New Delhi • Hong Kong • Buenos Aires

Designed by Maria Lilja
ISBN-13: 978-0-439-88470-9 • ISBN-10: 0-439-88470-5
Copyright © 2006 by Scholastic Inc.
All rights reserved. Printed in the U.S.A.

First printing, December 2006

12 11 10 9 8 7 6   8 9 10 11/0

Phonics Fact

Fl is a blend. Blends are two consonants whose sounds are blended together when you say them. You can hear the *fl* blend at the beginning of **fluffy**, **Flora**, **flamingo**, and **fly**. What other *fl* words can you find in this story? Look at the pictures, too!

Fluffy little **Flora Flamingo** cannot **fly.**

Every day, **Flora** tries to **fly** but fails.
Flap, flap, flap…**flop**. **Flap, flap, flap**…**flop**.

Flora is upset. She wants to **fly** to the **flamingo** festival in **Florida** with the rest of the **flamingo flock**.

I wish I could **fly** like the **butterflies** can **fly**.

Phonics Fact

Sometimes the *fl* blend comes in the middle of a word, as in **butterflies**. Can you spot another word in this story that has the *fl* blend in the middle?
(Answer: **fireflies**)

Flora watches the **butterflies**.
They **flutter** from **flower** to **flower**.

Flora tries to **fly** like the **butterflies**.
But it's no use.
Flap, flap, flap…**flop. Flap, flap, flap**…**flop**.

At night, **Flora** watches the **fireflies**. They **flicker** and **flash** as they **flit** through the air.

Flora tries to fly like the fireflies.
But it's no use.
Flap, flap, flap…flop. Flap, flap, flap…flop.

Flora's friend Floyd Flounder floats by.
"I'm a flop at flying," Flora tells Floyd.

"Just be patient," says **Floyd**. "Soon you will **fly** like the rest of the **flamingo flock**." **Flora** hopes **Floyd** is right.

One morning, **Flora** wakes up. Her **fluff** is gone!
Now she has **flashy** pink feathers!

Will the feathers help **Flora fly**?
Flap, flap, flap…

Flap, flap, flap, flap, flap, flap!
They do! **Flora** is not a **flop** at **flying** after all!

Soon it is time for all the **flamingos** to **fly** to **Florida**. Who will lead the **flock**? **Flora**, of course! And her **flying** is **FLAWLESS**!

FL Riddles

Listen to the riddles. Then match each riddle with the right *fl* word from the box.

> **Word Box**
> float   flamingo   flop   flapjack   flounder
> flowers   Florida   flash   flap   flock

1. You put these in a vase.

2. This kind of bird is big and pink.

3. A firefly's light does this at night.

4. This is a state in our country.

5. Boats do this on water.

6. It rhymes with *stop*.

7. This is what a group of birds is called.

8. It is another word for *pancake*.

9. This is a kind of fish.

10. Birds do this with their wings to fly.

FL Cheer

Hooray for *f-l*, the best sound around!

Let's holler *f-l* words all over town!

There's **flap** and **flop** and **flower** and **flu**.

There's **fluff** and **flamingo** and **flutter**, too!

There's **fly** and **flock** and **float** and **floor**.

There's **flute** and **flag** and many more!

F-l, f-l, give a great cheer,

For the most **flawless** sound you ever will hear!

Make a list of other *fl* words. Then use them in your cheer.

16